Heroes for Young Readers

Written by Renee Taft Meloche
Illustrated by Bryan Pollard

Gladys Aylward
Corrie ten Boom
William Carey
Amy Carmichael
Jim Elliot
Jonathan Goforth
Betty Greene
Adoniram Judson
Eric Liddell
David Livingstone
Lottie Moon
George Müller
Nate Saint
Mary Slessor
Hudson Taylor
Cameron Townsend

…and more coming soon.

Heroes for Young Readers are based on the *Christian Heroes: Then & Now* biographies by Janet and Geoff Benge. Don't miss out on these exciting, true adventures for ages ten and up! See the back of this book for a full listing of the biographies loved by children, parents, and teachers.

For a free catalog of books and materials contact
YWAM Publishing, P.O. Box 55787, Seattle, WA 98155
1-800-922-2143, www.ywampublishing.com

HEROES FOR YOUNG READERS

CAMERON TOWNSEND

Planting God's Word

Written by Renee Taft Meloche
Illustrated by Bryan Pollard

P.O. BOX 55787 SEATTLE, WA 98155

Cameron Townsend: Planting God's Word   Text © 2004 by Renee Taft Meloche   Illustrations © 2004 by Bryan Pollard
Published by YWAM Publishing, P.O. Box 55787, Seattle, WA 98155   ISBN 1-57658-241-8   Printed in China.   All rights reserved.

A boy named Cameron Townsend loved
        to figure out new things
like puzzles, riddles, mysteries
        that could be challenging.

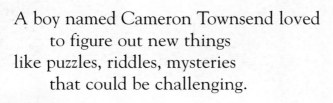

For Cam, as he was nicknamed, had
        a quick and eager mind.
He liked hard tasks that made him think
        whenever he had time.

But life was busy on his family's
        California farm.
Each morning Cam would feed and milk
        the cows out in the barn.

Cam helped his father plant and harvest
        barley and wild oats.
His family thanked God for their lives
        and were hard-working folks.

Each year, Cam watched as tiny seeds
    began to slowly grow.
They'd sprout and form green little buds
    and then, before you'd know,
they'd turn into tomatoes—fresh
    and juicy, ripe and red.
Cam's family, though they were quite poor,
    were healthy and well fed.

Cam's father read the Bible to
    his family every day.
They sang a hymn of praise and then
    together they would pray.

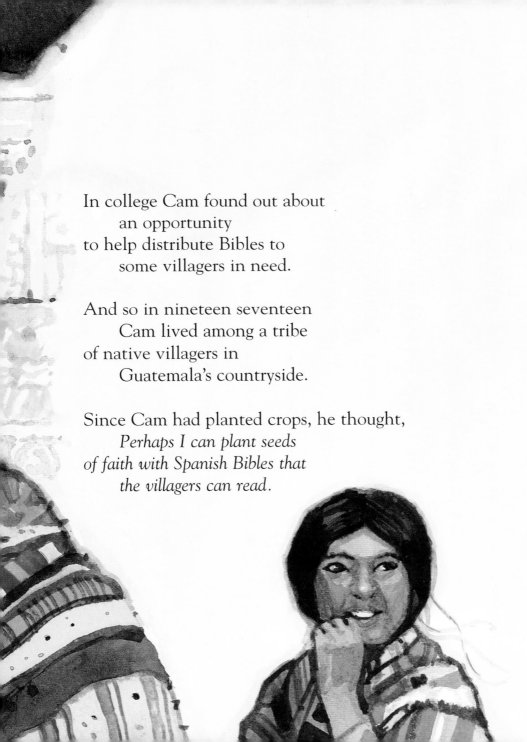

In college Cam found out about
    an opportunity
to help distribute Bibles to
    some villagers in need.

And so in nineteen seventeen
    Cam lived among a tribe
of native villagers in
    Guatemala's countryside.

Since Cam had planted crops, he thought,
    Perhaps I can plant seeds
of faith with Spanish Bibles that
    the villagers can read.

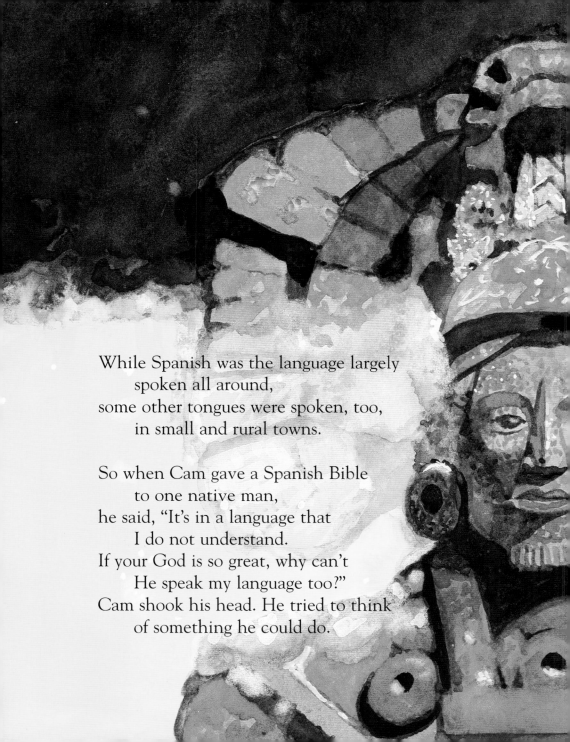

While Spanish was the language largely
    spoken all around,
some other tongues were spoken, too,
    in small and rural towns.

So when Cam gave a Spanish Bible
    to one native man,
he said, "It's in a language that
    I do not understand.
If your God is so great, why can't
    He speak my language too?"
Cam shook his head. He tried to think
    of something he could do.

He wanted them to read the Bible
  in their language, yet
no one had even started writing
  down their alphabet.

Cam wondered, *Could I manage to
  develop a good ear*
to hear their language, and then write
  it down so it is clear?

Cam used his gift for puzzles as
    he thought how to create
new letters that would represent
    the sound each one would make.

The Spanish alphabet, he soon
    decided, would work well.
He'd use the letters to make different
    words that they could spell.

So right away Cam set to work,
    from sunrise until dark,
till he could translate Bible chapters
    from the book of Mark.

And when Cam passed some chapters out,
    the people laughed and cried.
"God speaks our language!" they exclaimed
    with joy and newfound pride.

Cam built a school for those who wished
    to learn to read and write.
A power generator was
    installed to give them light.

Yet other tribes still had no written
    language of their own.
Cam needed to train others; he
    could not proceed alone.

He went to Arkansas, located
    in the southern States,
and formed a group called Wycliffe to
    teach others to translate.

Cam held two training camps, and he
    prepared recruits to go
to live among some native tribes
    in rural Mexico.

Cam drove himself there with a trailer
    to a tiny town.
Pigs scurried in the dust as barefoot
    children gathered round.

A short and square-faced man dressed in
    a cotton suit appeared.
He spoke to Cam in Spanish and
    said, "I'm the mayor here."

Cam knew the villagers there spoke
a language no one knew.
And so he told the mayor what
he hoped and planned to do.

"I'd like to learn your language and
then write it down for you."
The mayor smiled and said to Cam,
"You are most welcome to."

Cam parked his trailer in the square.
   The public came to see
just what this white man did inside.
   They loved especially
to watch Cam brush his teeth, a sight
   that they had never seen.
They ate a diet of tortillas,
   tadpoles, worms, and beans.

Cam made friends with the mayor and
        he read to him each day
some Spanish Bible chapters so
        he'd learn about God's ways.

The mayor's temper, though, had caused
        a lot of misery.
He'd done some things that were unfair
        and made some enemies.

Surprisingly, the mayor read
        the Bible right out loud
while standing in the square among
        a growing local crowd.

The mayor would translate the text
        so that they'd understand,
and then one day—quite puzzled—he
        spoke earnestly to Cam.

"A strange, strange thing has happened to
  me—it is something new.
I cannot seem to do the bad
  things I once used to do.
Whenever I'm about to drink
  too much or tell a lie,
there's something always stopping me.
  Can you please tell me why?"

Cam smiled and then replied to him,
  "God's Word is good and true,
and as you read about His ways,
  His love is changing you."

The mayor soon sent Bibles to
  his bitter enemies.
"This book makes me want to forgive,"
  he said. "Please read and see."

And while the mayor helped to share
    the Bible in that place,
Cam grew concerned about another
    need the people faced.

Their food lacked good nutrition; it
    was poor and incomplete.
They needed fruit and vegetables
    and more fresh food to eat.

Since Cam had planted crops before,
    he knew just how to sow.
He'd teach the villagers to plant
    new foods and make them grow.

Since topsoil that was needed had
    been used for bricks instead,
they took bat dung and ashes and
    some pig manure to spread
across the square, and then they helped
    to put in irrigation.
That way, fresh water could flow in
    throughout their vegetation.

Then in the city, Cam bought things
    that every garden needs:
some lettuce, carrot, celery,
    and beet and radish seeds.

The people tried imagining
    just how the plants would taste.
When harvest time arrived, Cam brought
    the children—eager-faced—
into the square to introduce
    new foods they would be fed.
He showed them how to pull up beets
    and cut up lettuce heads.

He sent them home with more fresh
    vegetables, and fruit as well.
Soon parents asked how they could grow
    them too—to eat and sell.

One day while Cam was weeding in
      a long row of green beans,
way at the far end of the square
      pulled up two limousines.

A chauffeur opened up a door.
      A famous face appeared—
the president of Mexico!
      What is he doing here?

The president shook hands with many
      villagers who came.
When Cam approached to shake his hand,
      he greeted Cam by name.

"I've heard about your work here and
      the good that you have done.
I wanted to inspect it and
      decided I would come."

Cam showed his language notes to him
out in the open air,
and then he told the president
of his true purpose there.

"Five hundred languages are still
unwritten in your land.
The Indians need people who
will work with them firsthand."

The president replied, "Would they
    make gardens like you do?"
Cam answered, "Si, señor, they'd gladly
    help with farming too."

The president looked most impressed
    and said, "Please bring them in.
This is exactly what we need.
    How soon can they begin?"

Just one week later trucks came to
    the village with supplies:
young fruit trees and a bull and cow—
    a wonderful surprise.

The government of Mexico
    donated other things:
a school, a playground, and some land
    to use for harvesting.

More Christians came to Mexico
    to live among the tribes
in distant mountain villages
    to help the people thrive.

Cam knew throughout the world, though, millions
    needed more to come
and help translate the Bible into
    their own special tongue.

Since then, two thousand Wycliffe workers
    have gone far and wide
so that God's love, through His true Word,
    may everywhere abide.

Cam died at eighty-five years old
        in nineteen eighty-two.
He planted seeds of faith in hearts;
        in soil, seeds that grew.

And still today God wants our help—
        the world is filled with needs—
and whether we plant crops or translate,
        we are sowing seeds.

Christian Heroes: Then & Now

by Janet and Geoff Benge

Heroes of History

by Janet and Geoff Benge

...and more coming soon. Unit study curriculum guides are also available.

For a free catalog of books and materials contact
YWAM Publishing, P.O. Box 55787, Seattle, WA 98155
1-800-922-2143, www.ywampublishing.com